Jethro Tull

FLUTE SOLOS

As Performed by
IAN ANDERSON

Transcribed by Jeff Rona

Cover photo: Fin Costello/Redferns

ISBN 978-1-4234-0977-9

HAL•LEONARD®
CORPORATION

7777 W. BLUEMOUND RD. P.O. BOX 13819 MILWAUKEE, WI 53213

Visit Hal Leonard Online at
www.halleonard.com

These solos are transcribed from the albums on which the songs may be found and, as such, are difficult to play (in true Ian Anderson intense, dynamic fashion). As the solos are excerpts from the complete pieces, they are often improvisational passages, containing different melodic ideas and voicings, and may not always include the original melody.

EXPLANATION OF THE FLUTE SYMBOLS

To achieve some of the techniques Ian Anderson employs on his flute we've added the following notations to the arrangements:

01	=	first harmonic
02	=	second harmonic
sing	=	sing into the flute
ord.	=	stop sing
fl.	=	flutter tongue
sing ∫	=	sing in the shape of the line
o ♪	=	increasing harmonics

The harmonics are achieved merely by overblowing until the next higher note (overtone) sounds. For the second harmonic, blow until the second higher note sounds. The increasing harmonics are achieved by gradually blowing harder and harder to get as many harmonics as possible.

Singing into the flute may be awkward at first. It is recommended that you learn the pieces first without the singing, then add the effect later. Sing the written note in the octave most comfortable for your voice. It is important to keep the airstream moving fast so there will be a good balance between flute and voice.

Ian Anderson has a distinct "dark" sound. In playing these pieces you may wish to play with the blow hole of your flute a little more covered than normal, and blow down into it more. The "dirty" passages should be played with a heavy tongue and almost overblown. You should, however, be careful not to let these techniques become habit.

CONTENTS

Baker St. Muse

Words and Music by
IAN ANDERSON

Big Dipper

Words and Music by
IAN ANDERSON

Bourée

Music by IAN ANDERSON

Bungle in the Jungle

Words and Music by
IAN ANDERSON

Chequered Flag
(Dead or Alive)

Words and Music by
IAN ANDERSON

Cross-Eyed Mary

Words and Music by
IAN ANDERSON

Cup of Wonder

Words and Music by
IAN ANDERSON

Fire at Midnight

Words and Music by
IAN ANDERSON

From Later

Words and Music by
IAN ANDERSON

Living in the Past

Words and Music by
IAN ANDERSON

Look into the Sun

Words and Music by
IAN ANDERSON

My God

Words and Music by
IAN ANDERSON

Nothing Is Easy

Words and Music by
IAN ANDERSON

Passion Play Edit #8

Words and Music by
IAN ANDERSON

Thick as a Brick

Words and Music by
IAN ANDERSON

Third Hurrah

Words and Music by
IAN ANDERSON

The Whistler

Words and Music by
IAN ANDERSON

42

The Witch's Promise

Words and Music by
IAN ANDERSON